LEARNING TO BE GRATEFUL WHEN WE'RE NOT THANKFUL

Oasis Center Library
317 East Call Street
Tallahassee, Florida 32301

Monekka L. Munroe

Learning To Be Grateful When We're Not Thankful

Copyright © 2015
Monekka L. Munroe

All rights reserved. No part of this book may be reproduced in any form without the expressed written permission of the publisher, except by a reviewer.

Great Minds Publishing
P.O. Box 5795
Tallahassee, Fl 32314

www.greatmindspublishing.com
greatmindspublishing@gmail.com

Printed in the USA
First Printing in 2015

Library of Congress Control Number: 2013941673
ISBN-10: 0989005011
ISBN-13: 978-0-9890050-1-2

Edited by Mrs. Aariel Simpkins
Cover Photo by Dr. James Moran
Hair by Mrs. Charmaine Williams-Davis

This book is dedicated to all women. Your best is good enough. You no longer need to seek validation from external forces. The God in each of us should be validation enough. Be proud of you, love you, and continue to build you.

Special Acknowledgements

For everything, I give all praises to the Creator who remains so merciful, loving, and forgiving. I will forever be grateful for my life, my family, friends, and enemies. Although all of my days are not sunny, I have learned to be both grateful and thankful for the opportunity to carry an umbrella during the storm.

Contents

Foreword — vi

Chapter 1 — 1
The Beauty of Being Broken

Chapter 2 — 5
Disturbing the Natural Order of Life

Chapter 3 — 9
Taking Ownership of Life Decisions

Chapter 4 — 12
Remember the Small Things

Chapter 5 — 15
Finding Your Voice:
The Courage to Say No

Chapter 6 — 22
A New Birth

Chapter 7 — 27
A Day of Rest

Foreword
Dianne Williams-Cox

It is with extreme honor and pleasure that I write this foreword for my "keeping it real" sister, Monekka! Our paths crossed at a point in life where we both were growing and going. She has been an awesome inspiration to me and my life as well as a strong mentor and supporter. Even though she is younger, I still consider her a mentor in that she does not let circumstances or people limit her progression to where God has already shown her that she is going.

This renowned author does not rest on her laurels and does not sit back and say…"I have mine…you've got to get yours!" She reaches back and brings people with her. She realizes that some of the people whom she brings may be grateful but not thankful. She also realizes that some of those people do not know their own self-worth or the talents that they possess. Monekka allow others to realize that if they will simply forgive themselves and move forward in life, the world will just have to deal with it.

I am truly grateful and thankful for meeting Monekka so many years ago. Interestingly enough, we met through both of us being of service to our community. I have never regretted our meeting that afternoon as we focused on her daughter. Her beautiful young lady was gathering information to enter my sorority's mentoring program. Through the love and guidance of her mother she completed our program with great success, and entered college where she was successful as well. I share this because as my grandmother often said, "Charity begins at home and goes abroad." Monekka takes care of home and whatever the world deals her. Her students absolutely adore her and I know from personal testimonies that their lives are forever changed after they leave her class.

I loved the last book and I know this one is also on its way to the top of the charts. You have experienced Oprah, but you have not lived until you have encountered Monekka!

Chapter One

The Beauty of Being Broken

The first time I felt the pain of heartbreak I thought it was the end of the world. For the longest time the only things I could focus on was the pain and feelings of being betrayed. The "why me" question continued to linger in my mind.

It never occurred to me until much later in life that pain is what makes us stronger, and it often teaches valuable life lessons about the wrong choices and mistakes we make. The ultimate lesson is finding and facing truth. Although there are times when truth isn't attractive, the benefit of that truth is where the attractiveness truly lies.

Often, a woman has to endure hardship or heartache before she realizes just how strong she is. Some women have endured abuse, divorce, financial downfalls, and so many other hurtful life situations. However, after the pain is gone, most women realize the beauty of being broken. There are many things in life that require being broken before their natural qualities of purity, goodness, and strength are exposed. Women are no different; because we are so loving, nurturing, and giving to others, there are times when we expose ourselves to pain and betrayal without thinking. More times than not, we are so focused on helping others that we let our guards down and forget to make sure that we are taking care of ourselves. Because of this, we are often viewed as weak, when in fact, we are stronger than we realize.

Twenty-six years ago, I was told that I did not have a stomach virus, nor were my symptoms the result of food poisoning, I was pregnant. I couldn't imagine how I would care for, or give a baby the things I knew it would need; at that time I didn't know how I would care for myself. I was devastated because I thought I didn't have anyone to help me. I didn't know where to turn, I was lost, afraid, and desperate. I was truly a broken woman. Before I gave birth, the only thing I had that was truly my own was a high school diploma. Really, that's all I had. I had no idea how strong, intelligent, and goal-driven I was, until my daughter was born.

I loved the innocence in her eyes and her beautiful smile. She worried about nothing. It seemed as if she knew I would make her world ok. I was determined to make sure she continued to feel safe in my arms and continued to trust that I would find a way. That was my moment.
The turning point took some time, but eventually I prepared myself to face some hard truths. First, I was not alone. There were plenty of people in my

life who were willing to help me. Second, I had to realize the power of helping myself, and last, I had to find the courage to let go of my fears. After many struggles and disappointments, I eventually enrolled and successfully graduated from college, began teaching at a university, married a wonderful man, and wrote a couple of books. I had to endure and embrace my lower points in life before I was able to envision, prepare, and put into action a plan to reach the high points.

Legendary football coach and author, Joe Taylor often says, "You have to win private battles before you can win public victories." As women, our private battles are those times when we feel as if we cannot be restored. Our private battles include feelings of loneliness, desertion, and defeat. All women have experienced at least one of these emotions, but before we can claim the victory, we must make every effort to prevent those moments from becoming a lifetime of brokenness. We also can't allow ourselves to feel guilty or embarrassed about any unfortunate situations that may have caused our pain. Every woman has made mistakes, even those who have yet to realize their mistakes.
Don't feel ashamed, learn the lessons and move forward gracefully. Don't beat yourself up and run away from life because of a bad decision (s); there are no perfect beings, and you are not alone.

As human beings we will endure some level of pain. Unfortunately, some of us are unwilling to make the sacrifices that will allow us to live pain-free. This process often means leaving something or someone behind. When the time is right, we have to make choices that will help us move forward instead of remaining in a place that will prevent us from moving at all.

Being broken must not become addictive. We should not search for situations or people who will continue to keep us stagnant. Women tend to repeat this cycle when dating. Some women will date the same type of men repeatedly, and never stop to think that these men are only treating them the way they allow themselves to be treated. These women have allowed the feeling of being broken to become an addictive way of living.

We have to accept the process of crawling before we can acknowledge the blessing of walking; being down should strengthen us as we prepare to celebrate the joy of being on the upside of a situation.

Chapter Two

Disturbing the Natural Order of Life

Every evening by 7:00, a small bird would fly to my back porch, perch himself on a ledge, and fall asleep. Because of its nightly visits, I named the bird Franklin. Each morning by 6:00, Franklin would fly away. I had no idea where he would go, but each evening he would faithfully return. A female friend suggested that I place some birdseeds in a bowl to feed him. WRONG!!!

That would have been a terrible thing to do. Franklin was surviving long before he found a resting place on my back porch. He knew to leave each morning to find food, and he knew exactly where to retrieve that food, and at the end of the day he returned to rest.

This is what most animals do, they do not require help from human beings to survive. However, isn't it funny that we recognize and accept this behavior as the norm for animals, yet we do not expect it from a man? The Bible says, "If any man is not willing to work, let him not eat." Yet, as women, we often disturb the natural order of life by interfering with those things that do not require our assistance.

I believe we should invest as much time in ourselves as we invest in others to ensure self-improvement, self-love, and self-appreciation. When we give so much of ourselves, it is usually in the form of supporting the dreams and aspirations of others. We support those we love, those we want to love us in return, and at times, those who refuse to pay any attention to us. The only individual who does not receive equal attention from us is us.

As a young girl, I was taught that being selfish was a bad characteristic to have. However, as a woman, I now know the importance of self-worth. We can't possibly care for others if we are not caring for ourselves appropriately. Our commitment to caring for others have caused more chaos than caring. Why? Because we often disturb the natural order of life.

As I carefully look at the present situation of some family dynamics, it seems as if a reversed phenomenon has occurred. Less than 20 years ago the man worked outside of the home to care and provide for his family and he did not complain about these duties. Because of this, he was deserving of what his wife provided for him in return. The wife or significant other cared for the children and took pride in making sure the house was a home. Most men came home to a clean house, dinner, and a happy family excited to welcome him home. Today however, those roles are reversed; there have been some dramatic changes in the family dynamics of this generation.

Today, the women are working outside of the home, caring for the home, the children, and the husband or boyfriend. Yet that same husband or boyfriend does not work at all. He provides no financial, emotional, or spiritual support. Along with providing no support, this man still expects home cooked meals, bills to be paid, and occasional sex. I'm not saying anything is wrong with this lifestyle if it works for the couple, I am simply making an observation. However, I am curious if this really "works" for any couple, or have women adjusted to this lifestyle because of their fear of being alone.

Over time, a lot of women have accepted as the norm some very different situations for the sake of maintaining a relationship with a man. For some reason the idea of a man embracing his role as the provider and protector of his family has slowly disappeared. However, if this relationship works for the couple and both are genuinely happy, then do what works.

Disturbing the natural order of life can also be the result of women who are disillusioned about the definition of being a nurturer. I know how good it feels to receive accolades for helping others and being that "go to" person, but being that individual at some point becomes draining. Once that feeling surfaces, some women will begin to feel bitter and disappointed because they have no one to depend on for strength and encouragement. This is an understandable feeling and women have the right to feel what they feel, but don't remain there. Use one of your arms, pat yourself on the back, look in the mirror and be proud of yourself. Use that moment to encourage yourself, pray for strength and determination, and move forward with life.

Do not disturb the natural order of what God has put in place. My life lesson was realizing that being a good woman does not mean being a crutch for others to lean on after convincing them that they no longer need their own legs to stand. We cannot save the world, actually we are not equipped to save anyone; it takes a lifetime to determine what it takes to save ourselves. I'm sure we all know some true superwomen in the world, but even those women need a break occasionally.

Chapter Three

Taking Ownership of Life Decisions

When unfortunate things happen in our lives it's much easier to place the blame on someone else. When we blame others, the responsibility of repairing our hurt is no longer ours and we begin to wait for someone else to step up and make life better for us. However, if we take ownership of the decisions we make, we are then forced to accept our role in the pain we feel.

Once accepted, we must begin the work of healing. This is by no means an easy road to travel. During this process, many emotions will show up to join our *pain party*. Feelings of guilt will surface, depression may visit, anger will attempt to stay long after the party is over, loneliness will definitely show up, and finally, peace-the party crasher. The day will come when we realize the pain is gone and we can start over. No one can release our pain, that task is ours. When we're ready to move forward, we will face our storm head on, determined to win.

A season has been designated for everyone. We do not have the capability to determine the date and time of our impending storm, but we do possess the capability to fight through it. We have to respect the season; it cannot be avoided, and it cannot be circumvented, it's all a part of the process of life.

The healing process takes time, patience, and much prayer. Heartache in particular takes the most time during the healing process. After feelings of betrayal are experienced, it's hard to look at life and people the same way. Many times we think that hurting others will minimize our pain or perhaps even make our pain go away. However, truthfully, hurting others will eventually cause us further pain. It's not worth it. During these times we should concentrate on healing ourselves and forget the idea of hurting others.

As I matured into a woman, I heard so many 'life gets better' phrases: Trouble don't last always; the sun always shines after a storm; tomorrow will be a brighter day, etc. Today, I realize the common theme of those phrases was simply to hold on and don't give up. That's what we must do during any trying situation. We must not give up and claim defeat so easily. Believe it or not, women were created to have a champion spirit, but there are times in life when our spirit becomes damaged and weakened by the decisions we make.

Now is the time to make decisions that will continue to strengthen not only our spirit but also the spirit of our sisters who have fallen and feel there is no other place for them except down. We are creatures of distinction, intelligence, empathy, and sympathy. We work hard, we are educated, dedicated, and we love with complete loyalty. Yet, with all of those beautiful characteristics, we are still human and we make mistakes.

Remember, life happens to the living! It does not matter how much education, money, or resources you have. It does not matter how loyal you are to friends and family, and it does not matter how much you attend church or pray. Life happens to everyone. What determines our level of strength is how we face those life situations. Don't give up. Many times we lose because we count ourselves out after realizing that others have given up on us. We cannot afford to give up on ourselves. We are worthy and we matter.

Chapter Four

Remember the Small Things

We often forget our "humble" beginnings, or if we do remember, they become extremely insignificant after we have reached some level of success. Unfortunately, we even forget about people after reaching levels of success. However, our beginnings can provide the blueprint for either a successful or disastrous ending. Either way, our beginnings should never be forgotten, but respected throughout the process of life.

Many times the ending is so much more enjoyable, and as a result, we don't recognize the need to be grateful for the beginning. I believe one reason for this is because so many of us struggle to move through the various phases of life and some of those struggles are so painful that we believe remembering will result in reliving painful experiences. I suppose at times this may be true, however, remembering our past can also help us to be both thankful and grateful for the present as well as create excitement about the future.

Before entering this phase of my life's journey, I can remember living in a two bedroom, single-wide trailer, driving a grey Dodge Omni.

I don't think those cars are even manufactured anymore! Nevertheless, my daughter and I would get into that car and drive everywhere! We didn't have a care in the world! I never imagined in a million years that I would one day drive another vehicle, purchase a home, and find peace along the way. Even before that journey, I can remember the times I had to walk or depend on public transportation. What I have since learned is my blessings began before the cars, apartments, and home ownership. The blessings began with my ability to walk to the bus stop, the ability to walk at all! The blessings began the moment I woke up to see another day and was able to work toward change.

In my opinion, blessings come in the form of things that we have absolutely no control of, things that cannot be explained. This is how I know God was then, as He is now, watching, forgiving, loving, and providing blessings the entire time. God does the things that cannot be explained, it is He who allows us to achieve the unachievable, God is the only one who can make believers of those who do not believe. As I continued to grow, continued to live, there was no explanation, no warning, only blessings.

Remembering those who helped or made sacrifices for us along our journey is also essential during our upward mobility. Whenever I hear people say,

"Nobody was there for me, I did this on my own," I immediately become nauseated. I don't know of any goal that can be achieved without the help of someone else. The problem we encounter many times is not being able to recognize help when it's given or offered. If it's not the kind of help we prefer, we reject it. So, when we can't get what we want, we become bitter, selfish, arrogant, and totally forget about the people who provided help in small ways. Those small ways may have included words of encouragement, prayers, a meal, providing transportation, or even subjecting us to tough love. Nevertheless, help was there and it played a significant role in the journey to success.

Chapter Five

Finding Your Voice: The Courage to Say No

How many times have we been asked to do something and we knew we should have said no? Instead, we said yes knowing disaster would be the end result. Why didn't we have the courage to say no? Is being a people pleaser synonymous with being a woman? Why is it that most of the people we attempt to please are usually the ones who care the least about us, or our efforts to make them happy?

What happens when we find our voice and scream as loudly as we can-NO?! No, we will not be there for you anymore. No, we will not do one last favor for you because all of those favors require spending money. No, we are not lonely, vulnerable beings who need to hear sweet lies to make us feel worthy. No, we are not free today to transport your children or other family members to doctor appointments, shopping trips, or anywhere else. No, we are not available to entertain trifling individuals whose only interest is to push deeper the knife that someone else left in our backs! No, we are no longer available!

However, to answer the question-*what would happen if we used our voices to say no*-the world would crumble! Yet, instead of crumbling the world, we would rather experience feelings of being crumbled instead. We have allowed ourselves to define womanhood as shouldering the problems of everyone else while putting our issues on the backburner, hoping that someday our problems will disappear. It doesn't have to be this way for women, it isn't mandated that we shoulder the problems of the world. We have the right to say no, and it's more than o.k. when we do.

Through many trials and tribulations, many women have discovered this secret. However, in order to be successful, women must also embrace the idea of living a life without apologies. This is difficult because we care so much about others, so much so that we would rather kidnap the pain, struggles, and burdens of someone else and bury our own pain. Believe it or not, we were taught this lesson at some point in our young lives. We have adopted this lesson and we're now teaching it to our daughters without a second thought. We have embraced the idea that being a superwoman is who we are at all times. We must display strength in everything we do, and this strength is often promoted by the false accolades we receive from others. The myth is we must stay strong, dedicated to satisfying the needs of others while remaining extremely quiet about our dissatisfaction of it all.

This superwoman concept is also the result of our lack of understanding and our inability as women to support each other. Often after we have encountered the beginning of our storm, we look for support and encouragement from our female friends. However, at times, we leave feeling worse than we did before reaching out for help. The one phrase that offers no support but seems to be the most popular is, "Girl, things could be a lot worse."

When a woman is hurt or confused, she is not worrying about or comparing her situation to someone else. Furthermore, her feelings should not be minimized by reminding her that "it could be worse." Where she is at that moment, and the way she feels during that time is important to her, and more than anything it should be understood that she has the right to feel the way she feels.

What exactly does that phrase mean? Should women wait until they are almost dead before they have the right to feel pain or moments of weakness? Are we supposed to be lost in the wilderness before receiving permission to experience mental stress? This is one of the disadvantages of being perceived as a strong woman or a woman who has it together. People will assume that we should bounce back immediately from a fall or perhaps have no feelings at all, which could also be the main reason they feel comfortable overwhelming us with their life struggles.

You are superwoman! How dare you cry or feel emotionally weak, you are made of steel! How dare you feel as if you are losing ground; how dare you feel like a failure! Your shoulders are unbreakable! How dare you come to me for comfort! How dare you! You are a robot; you have no feelings, no emotions. Your primary job is to stay strong and be there for me when I fall. You see, I am human; I have the right to hurt, cry, scream, fall, feel weak, and at times want to give up. However, you're superwoman, and you are no longer entitled to these feelings. Know your place!

This is the message we give when we lack the necessary support needed to build each other up. Because of this indirect message, women often find it difficult to say no to the needs of others. This is extremely unhealthy, and this brings absolutely no value to our personal lives. We want so badly to be perceived as good women, loyal women who know how to treat others. This perception keeps us in bondage and enslaved to the needs of others.

As women, must help each other by reviving our spirits to live. Together we can jump start the needed motivation to continue the fight and survive. Let's begin speaking life into our sisters instead of beating them down or taking their pain to other circles that will use that pain to cause further hurt.

Our friends come to us because they believe they can trust us with their hearts, secrets, joys, and their pain. Just because we may disagree with their life decisions doesn't mean we should take on the "I told you so" attitude if the decision results in disappointment. It also doesn't mean that we should seek out the people who never cared for our friend to share her business with. In instances such as these, we are selfishly seeking someone else to validate our reasons for disagreeing with our friend's life choices. If you can talk honestly to others about the business of your friend, shouldn't you be able to speak just as honestly to your friend? Remember, we all have been there; all women have experienced the need for a shoulder to cry on or simply an ear to listen. Help our sisters regain their self-confidence, help them find their voice.

Finding our voices however, can cost us greatly. It is shameful to hear the names we are called after we realize our worth, our rights, the power of our voice. We are often called a bitch, accused of not knowing our place or having a bad attitude, and at times, we are even belittled by being told that women of other ethnicities are better women than we are. We essentially risk being no better than garbage when we decide to say no to everyone else, and yes to ourselves.

Nevertheless, we must find and recognize that power. We can no longer allow others to silence us in order to keep them comfortable. If our voice and our truth cause others to stir in their seats, then they should move. I can remember being employed at various agencies and speaking against issues such as racial or gender biases that were extremely prevalent. Some of the other employees would sit with me behind closed doors to complain about being mistreated or overlooked for promotion opportunities. However, during staff meetings where they should have felt free to voice their concerns, those same employees remained as quiet as a church mouse in the presence of supervisors. They felt more comfortable talking behind closed doors about their problems, but being behind closed doors did not provide a solution.

There were other times when I was reminded of potential consequences for speaking out, even if the truth was being spoken! However, I never allowed threats or consequences to stop me. I would often remember the courageous women who stood and sacrificed before, yet for me. Suppose great women such as Mary McCloud Bethune, Shirley Chisholm, Fannie Lou Hamer, Sojourner

Truth, Harriet Tubman, and Ida B. Wells had allowed the fear of consequences to silence them, how many opportunities would we lack if these women did not speak up? Recognize the power of your voice-SPEAK!

Chapter Six

A New Birth

Although the Father of the heavens and earth has the ability to speak life into the dead, He has given His children the ability to speak into existence the life we desire, even when death surrounds us.
-Author

Starting over is similar to a new birth, and life will require starting over from time to time. Some may need a new start after separating from a loved one, some are forced to start over after the death of a family member or friend, and for others a fresh start may simply mean leaving one career to begin another. Whatever the reason, starting over can be an essential part of discovering that missing piece of life's puzzle that is needed to make one complete.

The courage to take the plunge is another beast. Just like the beginning of a new birth, deciding to move forward can be scary, painful, unknowing, and lonely. The decision to start over can be extremely ugly! There will be times when no one understands or perhaps question your decision, and others may even try to convince you that you are making the biggest mistake of your life. All of that is o.k., what's important is your understanding of the drive and motivation to seek and move toward your destiny. As long as you understand how, when, and why, nothing else matters.

Before the actual birth of a child, the body experiences a series of uncontrollable pain, often referred to as labor pains. These pains alert us to the arrival of our new bundle of joy, a baby boy or girl, a new life. The labor pains of life have the same meaning. When we experience a feeling that we cannot explain or the desire to find that missing piece, this marks the beginning of those pains. Something deep inside of us is pushing us to be better! This is the point where we must decide to act on those impulses, determine who should come with us, and those who will be left behind. This is very difficult; the pain of leaving something or someone behind is not easy, even if the only thing you are neglecting is your comfort zone.

In 1996, I moved from Gainesville, FL to Tallahassee, FL to attend college. I was so scared! I had no idea what to expect, I was afraid of the people, I didn't want to talk to anyone, I was a nervous wreck! However, before deciding to leave Gainesville, there was a feeling inside of me that would not go away! I was becoming increasingly unhappy living there but couldn't identify a specific reason why. The only thing I knew for sure was I needed to move. Once I relocated to Tallahassee, I wanted to return home. Not because I missed home, but because home was what I knew, I was comfortable there, I knew people, places, and things, yet that was also the place where I experienced a lot of unhappiness.

After months of keeping myself busy with my daughter, schoolwork, meeting new people, working, and volunteering in the community, I decided to stay. It was one of the best decisions I'd ever made. I secured a dynamic education, career, met lifelong friends, and discovered a passion for helping those less fortunate or overlooked by society. I found a piece of my life's puzzle that was missing for a very long time. The anxiety I felt about leaving Gainesville, the uncertainty, and even wanting to return to my comfort zone were my life's labor pains preparing me for the new life that I would live. Every doubt or sleepless night was so worth it. I was truly happy and couldn't imagine leaving or desiring anything more. At least that's what I thought.

In 2014, I felt the itch once more. I was feeling bored in Tallahassee, the excitement I once felt was gone. I no longer enjoyed going to the places that I once frequented, I found myself living a rigid daily routine of work, research, and home. I couldn't understand this strange, yet familiar feeling. It was strange because on the outside it looked as if I had it all; I was living in a beautiful gated community, I was recently promoted to an assistant professor at a local university, and recently purchased my dream car. Why wouldn't I be happy in this place? However, this feeling was familiar because I felt the same way before leaving Gainesville. In 2015, I made a very tough decision. After many discussions with the department chair at the university where I was employed, I resigned. I decided to leave; not only did I leave Tallahassee, I left Florida. That was a bold move!

Through tears and confusion, I tried hard to explain my decision to family members and close friends. I tried to explain that I knew for sure there was something else out there for me, something I could not explain, a feeling that would not go away. Although I could not tell them what was waiting for me, I knew for sure that I would not be able to find it by staying still, by holding on to familiar surroundings, by being comfortable. I was leaving my comfort zone yet again, traveling to take advantage of the unknown. I was now unemployed with limited finances. I can admit without shame that the more I tried to explain my desire to start over, the crazier I sounded! That is how I knew God was truly in control, and it was He who was guiding my steps because what God has for us cannot be explained. It cannot be explained because His favor requires no explanation. Our job is to be patient and obedient.

Patience was then and still is, very difficult for me. There are many things I wish to have right now, but I believe God for who He is. Once again, I have decided to step out on faith with the belief that I will be o.k. I am prepared for the labor pains of life because I know without any doubt that a new life awaits me yet again. No pain, no gain.

Chapter Seven

A Day of Rest

So the people rested on the seventh day.
Exodus 16:30

My grandmother would often say, "People need to slow down and smell the roses sometime. Life ain't that serious."

Each week I choose a day to rest. I turn off the computer, my cell phone, the radio, the television, and I do not answer my door. The entire day is for rest. Life requires rest from people, places, and things. It helps to restore and maintain the physical and mental energy required to deal with life. Our day of rest should not be filled with guilt or thoughts of what we could be doing, or what we should do the following day. Our day of rest should be about rest.

Suggesting the idea of doing nothing to certain people is an insult. One of my very dear friends believed in working every day of the week without a break. This friend wasn't able to see the value in resting. Instead, the focus of his value was going into the office, turning on the computer, answering emails, returning calls, and scheduling trips to attend conferences. The switch did not turn on until I presented a gentle reminder. I told my friend that even God saw the need for a break. The Creator of the universe worked hard for six days creating the entire world yet on the seventh day, He recognized the need to rest. I am quite sure no one is building an entire universe that could overshadow the world God has created.

There are many ways to rest physically and mentally, the choice is ours. Meditation is the most effective way for me. Sitting quietly in a space of tranquility, being able to concentrate, pray, allowing myself to become one with the Creator and nature.

We should take pride in caring for our mind and body. We must make it a priority because a sane mind is capable of manifesting greatness wherever we are. A healthy mind and body helps us maintain our vision of viewing life as unlimited possibilities instead of perceiving it as numerous liabilities.

Resting is spending valuable time with ourselves, learning to be grateful, even when we're not thankful.